Unsolved!

MYSTERIES OF THE BERMUDA TRIANGLE

Kathryn Walker

based on original text by Brian Innes

Crabtree Publishing Company

www.crabtreebooks.com

Crabtree Publishing Company

www.crabtreebooks.com

Author: Kathryn Walker
    based on original text by Brian Innes
Project editor: Kathryn Walker
Picture researcher: Rachel Tisdale
Managing editor: Miranda Smith
Art director: Jeni Child
Design manager: David Poole
Editorial director: Lindsey Lowe
Children's publisher: Anne O'Daly
Editor: Molly Aloian
Proofreaders: Ellen Rodger, Crystal Sikkens
Project coordinator: Robert Walker
Production coordinator: Katherine Berti
Prepress technician: Katherine Berti

The Brown Reference Group plc
First Floor
9-17 St. Albans Place
London N1 0NX
www.brownreference.com

Copyright © 2008 The Brown Reference Group plc

Photographs:
Cody Images: p. 4, 18
Corbis: p. 13, 15, 20
Fortean Picture Library: p. 6, 30;
    Andrew C. Stewart: p. 22
Bruce Gernon: p. 25
Istockphoto: Bill Koplitz: p. 27
NASA: p. 9
NOAA: p. 14, 28, 29
Shutterstock: David Brimm: p. 21;
    Ivan Cholakov: p. 12; Elen: p. 24;
    W. Holger: p. 8; Nikolay Okhitin: p. 26;
    Spectral Design: p. 16; T-Design: cover
U.S. Navy: p. 10

Illustration:
Stefan Chabluk: p. 7

Every effort has been made to trace the
owners of copyrighted material.

Library and Archives Canada Cataloguing in Publication

Walker, Kathryn, 1957-
    Mysteries of the Bermuda Triangle / Kathryn Walker ; based
on original text by Brian Innes.

(Unsolved!)
Includes index.
ISBN 978-0-7787-4144-2 (bound).--ISBN 978-0-7787-4157-2 (pbk.)

    1. Bermuda Triangle--Juvenile literature. I. Innes, Brian II. Title.
III. Series: Unsolved! (St. Catharines, Ont.)

G558.W34 2008   j001.94   C2008-904327-8

Library of Congress Cataloging-in-Publication Data

Walker, Kathryn, 1957-
  Mysteries of the Bermuda Triangle / Kathryn Walker based on original text by
Brian Innes.
      p. cm. -- (Unsolved!)
    Includes index.
    ISBN-13: 978-0-7787-4157-2 (pbk. : alk. paper)
    ISBN-10: 0-7787-4157-5 (pbk. : alk. paper)
    ISBN-13: 978-0-7787-4144-2 (reinforced library binding : alk. paper)
    ISBN-10: 0-7787-4144-3 (reinforced library binding : alk. paper)
    1. Bermuda Triangle--Juvenile literature. I. Innes, Brian Bermuda Triangle. II. Title.

G558.W35 2009
001.94--dc22
                                              2008030110

Crabtree Publishing Company

www.crabtreebooks.com   1-800-387-7650
Copyright © **2009 CRABTREE PUBLISHING COMPANY.**

Published in Canada
Crabtree Publishing
616 Welland Ave.
St. Catharines, ON
L2M 5V6

Published in the United States
Crabtree Publishing
PMB 59051
350 Fifth Avenue, 59th Floor
New York, New York 10118

Printed in the USA/032010/CG20100208

Contents

The Mystery of Flight 19

...In 1945, a group of planes vanished off the coast of Florida.

It was a clear December afternoon in Fort Lauderdale, Florida. Five U.S. Navy **bombers** took off together. The flight was a **training exercise**. It was listed as Flight 19.

At about 3:45 p.m. there was a radio call from the pilot leading the group. He had lost his way. Sometime between 6 p.m. and 7 p.m., all five planes disappeared and were never seen again.

At first, people thought the planes had run out of fuel and crashed into the water. In the 1950s and 1960s, journalists claimed that something more mysterious had happened. Books and articles linked Flight 19 with other strange disappearances in the same area.

>> **bomber** — An aircraft that drops bombs

One of the rescue planes searching for Flight 19 disappeared, too.

No wreckage of Flight 19 or the rescue plane has ever been found.

"People thought the planes had run out of fuel and crashed..."

These are U.S. Navy Avenger bombers. In 1945, a group like this vanished without a trace.

A Deadly Triangle

...Many strange things happened in the same stretch of water.

Vincent Gaddis was a journalist. In 1964, he wrote an article named *The Deadly Bermuda Triangle*. It was about ships, planes, and **crews** that had vanished mysteriously. They had all disappeared in the same area of the Atlantic Ocean.

This area lay between Bermuda, Miami, and Puerto Rico. Drawing a line between these three places makes a perfect triangle. Gaddis called this "The Bermuda Triangle."

Gaddis believed that there were too many disappearances in the Triangle for it to be chance. If this was true, then what strange **forces** were at work in the Bermuda Triangle?

These are some of the books written about the Bermuda Triangle. Millions of copies have been sold around the world.

>> **crew** — People working on board a ship or aircraft

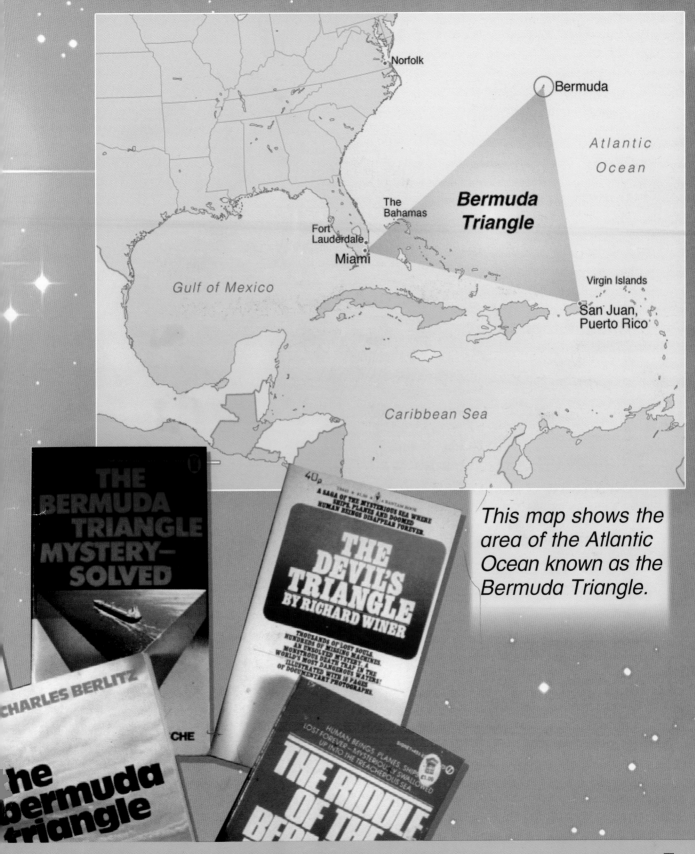

Norfolk

Bermuda

Atlantic Ocean

The Bahamas

Bermuda Triangle

Fort Lauderdale

Miami

Gulf of Mexico

Virgin Islands

San Juan, Puerto Rico

Caribbean Sea

THE BERMUDA TRIANGLE MYSTERY— SOLVED

40p
A SAGA OF THE MYSTERIOUS SEA WHERE
SHIPS, PLANES AND DOOMED
HUMAN BEINGS DISAPPEAR FOREVER.

THE DEVIL'S TRIANGLE BY RICHARD WINER

THOUSANDS OF LOST SOULS.
HUNDREDS OF MISSING MACHINES.
AN UNSOLVED MYSTERY! A
MONSTROUS DEATH TRAP IN THE
WORLD'S MOST DANGEROUS WATERS!
ILLUSTRATED WITH 16 PAGES
OF DOCUMENTARY PHOTOGRAPHS.

CHARLES BERLITZ

CHE

he bermuda triangle

HUMAN BEINGS, PLANES, SHIPS
LOST FOREVER—MYSTERIOUSLY SWALLOWED
UP INTO THE TREACHEROUS SEA

THE RIDDLE OF THE

This map shows the area of the Atlantic Ocean known as the Bermuda Triangle.

>> **force** — Someone or something with great power or strength

Old Sea Stories

Christopher Columbus was a famous **explorer**. In 1492, he sailed from Spain across the Atlantic Ocean.

Columbus' three ships sailed through the Sargasso Sea. This is a huge area of the Atlantic Ocean. Part of it is inside the Bermuda Triangle.

Columbus wrote about strange things that happened in the Sargasso Sea. He once saw a ball of fire fall into the water. He said that the ship's **compasses** did not work normally in that area.

One night, Columbus and his crew saw a light in the distance. It flickered like a candle, but they were nowhere near land. The sailors never discovered where the light came from.

The ship in this picture is a copy of the Santa Maria. *This was the ship that carried Columbus across the Atlantic Ocean in 1492.*

>> **explorer** — Someone who travels to find out about distant or new places

A Dangerous Place

For hundreds of years afterward, sailors told stories about what could happen in the mysterious waters. Some of the stories were true. Many ships were lost in storms there. Others were captured by pirates.

In the 1950s and 1960s, people began to count the ships and planes that had disappeared in the Atlantic Ocean. Many books and articles were written about the area that was now known as the Bermuda Triangle.

This is the surface of the Sargasso Sea. The sea is named for the Sargassum that floats there. This is a type of dark green or brown seaweed.

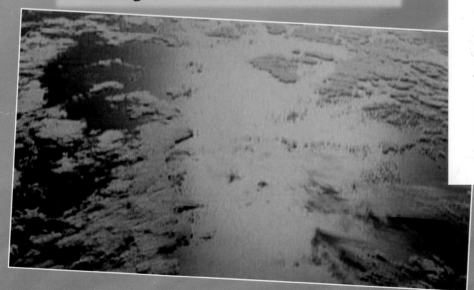

How Strange...

- Huge mats of seaweed float on the surface of the Sargasso Sea.

- There is often no wind on the Sargasso Sea. Sailing ships can be stuck there for weeks.

- Columbus is not the only person to have had difficulties with compasses inside the Bermuda Triangle. Other pilots and sailors have reported similar problems.

>> **compass** — An instrument used by sailors to show direction

Vanishing Ships

...In 1918, one of the U.S. Navy's largest ships went missing.

On March 4, 1918, the USS *Cyclops* left Barbados in the Caribbean. The ship was on its way to Norfolk, Virginia. Somewhere inside the Bermuda Triangle, *Cyclops* vanished. It was carrying radio equipment. Nobody received a call for help from the ship.

The U.S. was at war with Germany at the time *Cyclops* disappeared. It is possible that a German submarine or **battleship** attacked and sunk *Cyclops*.

Perhaps a **hurricane** caused the ship to sink. No one knows for sure what happened to the *Cyclops*. There were 306 crew and passengers on board. They all disappeared with the ship.

>> **battleship** — A large warship armed with guns

This picture of the USS *Cyclops* was taken in 1911. It was carrying heavy cargo at the time it went missing. This may have caused the ship to overturn in strong winds.

"Somewhere inside the Bermuda Triangle, Cyclops vanished."

>> **hurricane** — A violent, tropical storm with very strong winds

Vanishing Sisters

Cyclops, *Proteus*, and *Nereus* were all **sister ships**. *Cyclops* went missing in 1918. Then, 23 years later, disaster struck again.

On November 3, 1941, *Proteus* set off from St. Thomas in the Virgin Islands. The ship was sailing to Norfolk, Virginia, but it never arrived.

On December 10, 1941, *Nereus* set off on the same journey. It vanished without a trace, too. Like *Cyclops*, both ships disappeared somewhere in the Bermuda Triangle.

This is St. Thomas in the Virgin Islands. Ships traveling between the island and the U.S. have to pass through the Bermuda Triangle.

"On November 3, 1941, *Proteus* set off from St. Thomas..."

>> **sister ships** — Ships of the same type and age

War Victims?

Both *Proteus* and *Nereus* had been carrying **bauxite**. Bauxite is a rock that contains the metal aluminum. This is important for making aircraft.

At the time of the disappearances, the U.S. was building many aircraft. World War II was being fought throughout Europe. The U.S. was supplying aircraft to countries who were fighting Germany.

The U.S. Navy thought it was likely that *Proteus* and *Nereus* had been sunk by a German submarine. Wreckage from the ships has never been found.

This diver is exploring a wreck off the Bahamas. Maybe one day the wreckage of Proteus *and* Nereus *will be discovered.*

>> **bauxite** — A soft rock that is the major source of aluminum

"There can be very violent storms..."

More Losses

On April 5, 1950, the **cargo ship** *Sandra* went missing on a voyage through the Bermuda Triangle. There was a radio on board, but no one used it to call for help. Once again, a ship and her crew had mysteriously disappeared.

In October 1951, a ship named *Southern Districts* was lost. It was last seen in stormy seas close to the Bermuda Triangle. In 1955, a life preserver carrying the ship's name turned up off the Florida coast. It was all that was ever found of the ship and her crew.

At the center of this photograph, you can see storm clouds over the Bermuda Triangle. Such storms may haved caused many ships to sink.

>> **cargo ship** — A ship or vessel that carries goods and materials.

Stormy Seas

Many other ships have vanished in the Bermuda Triangle. The crews of some of them were rescued. They said that bad weather had damaged their ships.

There can be very violent storms in this part of the Atlantic Ocean. Some people believe that these storms are the reason for the large number of disappearances in the Bermuda Triangle.

*This poster shows a drawing of the **yacht** Saba Bank. The yacht went missing in the Bermuda Triangle on March 10, 1974.*

Ghost Ships

...Ships have been found drifting in the Triangle with no crew on board.

In 1881, the ship *Ellen Austin* was sailing south of Bermuda. It came across an unnamed ship that was drifting. There was no sign of her crew.

The captain of *Ellen Austin* ordered some of his seamen on board this ship. He told them to sail her into **port**. The captain would receive payment for bringing the ship back safely.

The two ships lost sight of each other for a while. A few days later, the crew of *Ellen Austin* spotted the unnamed ship again. To their horror, they saw there was no one on board. There was no sign of their shipmates.

>> **port** — Town with a harbor or place where ships can shelter

"To their horror, the crew saw there was no one on board."

How Strange...

In 1955, the yacht *Connemara IV* was found drifting south of Bermuda. The crew had vanished.

In 1948 the yacht and lifeboat of jockey **Al Snyder** were found in the Triangle. There was no trace of Snyder or of his two companions.

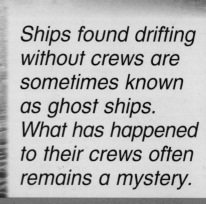

Ships found drifting without crews are sometimes known as ghost ships. What has happened to their crews often remains a mystery.

>> **jockey** — Someone who rides horses in races

Vanishing Planes

...The planes on Flight 19 were not the only ones lost inside the Bermuda Triangle.

The *Star Tiger* was a British passenger plane. On January 29, 1948, it set off on the last leg of its flight to Bermuda. Somewhere between 3:15 p.m. and 3:50 a.m. *Star Tiger* went missing. It seemed to simply vanish from the sky.

How could this have happened? *Star Tiger* was carrying a full load of fuel. Its crew was very **experienced**. The strangest thing of all was that no one had radioed for help.

People investigating the disappearance said they were completely puzzled. They said that what happened to *Star Tiger* was "an **unsolved** mystery."

>> **experienced** — Having skill or knowledge from doing something many times

In January 1949, the airliner *Star Ariel* vanished as mysteriously as *Star Tiger*. It was also lost in the Bermuda Triangle.

"...*Star Tiger*... seemed to simply vanish from the sky."

This is an Avro Tudor IV passenger aircraft. It was the same type of plane as the Star Tiger *and* Star Ariel.

These passengers are boarding a plane to Miami. The year is 1950. Two years earlier a similar flight ended in mystery.

Douglas DC-3

Less than a year after *Star Ariel* vanished, another passenger plane went missing.

On the evening of December 27, 1948, an old Douglas DC-3 aircraft left Puerto Rico. It was flying 27 passengers to Miami. The pilot radioed Miami just before dawn. He said they were 50 miles (80 km) away. But the plane was never heard from again.

It is possible that the pilot made a mistake about his position. The wind had changed direction. This could have blown the plane **off course**. Then it may have crashed into the Gulf of Mexico. No one looked for the plane there.

How Strange...

In 1951, a U.S. Air Force plane crashed about 2,000 miles (3,220 km) north of Bermuda. Some books say it was lost in the Bermuda Triangle.

>> **off course** — Not moving in the right direction

The Triangle Grows Bigger

Books have listed many other planes lost in the Bermuda Triangle. However, some of them actually disappeared thousands of miles away.

To include these stories, **authors** and journalists have widened the area they write about. Some have added the Gulf of Mexico. Others have added most of the northwest Atlantic Ocean.

Look at the map on page 7. You will see that these areas are a long way outside the area between Bermuda, Miami, and Puerto Rico.

This is southern Florida seen from the air. It is where the pilot of the lost DC-3 hoped to land in December, 1948. Instead the plane disappeared.

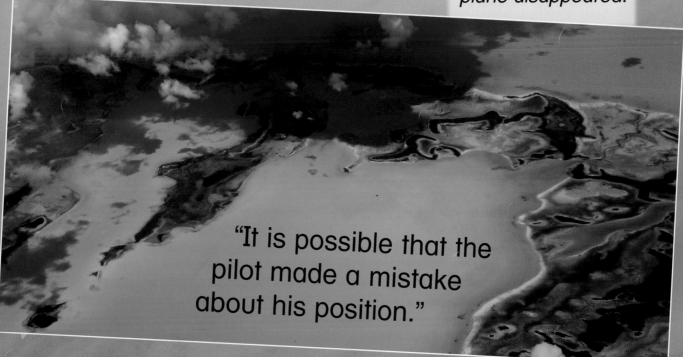

"It is possible that the pilot made a mistake about his position."

What is the Truth?

...People have found many ways to explain the strange events in the Bermuda Triangle.

Charles Berlitz was a language expert and a writer. In 1974 he wrote a book about the Bermuda Triangle. It sold millions of copies. Berlitz said it was as if the lost ships and planes had been snatched into another time or place.

According to **legend**, there was once a great island named Atlantis. It sank into the ocean thousands of years ago. Berlitz thought Atlantis was near the island of Bimini in the Bahamas. This is in the western corner of the Triangle.

Berlitz wondered if something remained of that powerful **civilization**. If it did, perhaps it had something to do with the disappearances.

>> **legend** — A story handed down from generation to generation

How Strange...

▷ In 1968, strange stones were found off the island of Bimini in the Bahamas. Some people think these are ruins of Atlantis.

"... Atlantis...sank into the ocean thousands of years ago."

This is an artists idea of what the city on the sunken island of Atlantis looks like.

>> **civilization** — A highly organized society, or group of people

Spacecraft and Aliens

Some people believe there is a hole or passageway in the Bermuda Triangle. They think it leads to other times or places. Maybe this is where the missing ships and planes have gone.

People have suggested that **alien** spacecraft are using this passageway to land on Earth. They say that aliens could be capturing the crews of planes and ships.

This is an artist's idea of what the alien spacecrafts look like. Some people believe that aliens have something to do with strange events in the Bermuda Triangle.

In 1971, the crew of the USS *John F. Kennedy* saw a huge glowing **object** hovering above them. This happened when the ship was inside the Bermuda Triangle.

>> **alien** — A creature from another planet

"A strange cloud surrounded his plane."

Tunnel in the Clouds

On December 4, 1970, Bruce Gernon was flying from the Bahamas to Florida. A strange cloud surrounded his plane.

A small tunnel opened in the cloud. Bruce flew through the tunnel toward the blue sky ahead. Suddenly, the plane seemed to move very fast. The compass was spinning.

When his plane came out of the tunnel, Bruce could see Miami Beach ahead. The flight had taken just 47 minutes. It usually took 75 minutes. Bruce could not make sense of what happened that day.

This is what Bruce Gernon described seeing as he flew through the strange cloud tunnel.

>> **hovering** — Floating in the air over something or someone

This is a magnetic compass. Normally, a compass needle points to the north.

Compass Problems

Some ships and planes have had trouble with their compasses while traveling inside the Bermuda Triangle. What could be causing this?

Magnetic energy is a force, or power. It pulls one object toward another object. Earth acts like a large **magnet**. It pulls the needle of a magnetic compass toward the north. This is how a compass helps travelers find their way.

But there are things that cause a compass needle to turn away from the north. Special types of rock can make this happen. Lightning or an undersea earthquake can make it happen, too. Maybe conditions in the Triangle are affecting compasses. This could have caused some disasters.

"Maybe conditions in the Triangle are affecting compasses."

How Strange...

The pilot leading Flight 19 *(see page 4)* reported compass problems.

Bruce Gernon said that his compass needle was spinning when he traveled through the cloud tunnel *(see page 25)*.

>> **magnet** — An object that can attract iron or steel

Gas Attack?

Scientists have discovered large amounts of gas trapped in the ocean floor of the Bermuda Triangle. This is gas is called **methane**. An earthquake under the sea could release it.

If a huge bubble of gas rose to the surface, it would produce a dip in the water. A ship that fell into this dip would sink quickly.

A gas bubble rising into the air could destroy passing aircraft. It could cause engines to fail. Or it could cause an explosion.

Lightning can cause problems with electrical equipment and compasses. It can also cause explosions in aircraft and ships.

>> **methane** — A colorless, odorless gas that catches fire easily

Wild Weather

The Bermuda Triangle is known for its sudden and fierce storms. The weather there can change quickly and without warning. Sailors have always feared the area because of this.

Hurricanes often happen in the Bermuda Triangle. These are strong winds that move at very high speeds.

Some people have seen a strange **yellow** fog **in the Bermuda Triangle.**

One pilot said that his electrical equipment failed while he was in this yellow fog. Also, his compass was spinning round and round.

Many ships in the Bermuda Triangle may have been lost because of very rough waters.

>> **fog** — A very thick mist that makes it hard to see

"...Tornadoes...often create waterspouts in the Bermuda Triangle."

Weird Waterspouts

Tornadoes are swirling winds. A **waterspout** happens when a tornado pulls water up into the sky. Tornadoes often create waterspouts in the Bermuda Triangle.

This weird weather can destroy or damage ships and aircraft. It could explain many disappearances inside the Bermuda Triangle.

A waterspout can pull water thousands of feet into the sky.

Explaining the Mystery

We can explain most of the disappearances in the Bermuda Triangle. Some of the missing ships were old or carrying too much cargo. The area has sudden storms and strange weather. People make mistakes. All these things can cause disasters.

It is true that many planes and ships have been lost in the Bermuda Triangle. But the area has a lot of **traffic**. A large number of ships and planes cross the Bermuda Triangle safely. Compared to this, the number of losses does not seem unusually high.

Some events still remain hard to explain. Books about the Bermuda Triangle have added to the sense of mystery. The facts are often wrong or important information is left out. This can make the facts seem more strange.

A lot of people enjoy reading about strange and unexplained things. This keeps alive the mystery of the deadly Bermuda Triangle.

The author of this book claims that there are simple explanations for most of the disappearances in the Triangle.

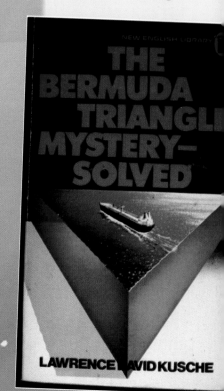

>> **traffic** —Vehicles, such as ships, traveling along a route

Glossary

alien A creature from another planet

author Someone who writes books or other text, such as essays or poems

battleship A large warship armed with guns

bomber An aircraft that drops bombs

bauxite A soft rock that is the major source of aluminum

cargo ship A ship or vessel that carries goods and materials

civilization A highly organized society, or group of people

compass An instrument used by sailors to show direction

crew People working on board a ship or aircraft

experienced Having skill or knowledge from doing something many times

explorer Someone who travels to find out about distant or new places

fog A very thick mist that makes it hard to see

force Someone or something with great power or strength

hovering Floating in the air over something or someone

hurricane A violent, tropical storm with very strong winds

jockey Someone who rides horses in races

legend A story handed down from generation to generation

magnet An object that can attract iron or steel

methane A colorless, odorless gas that catches fire easily

off course Not moving in the right direction

port Town with a harbor or place where ships can shelter

sister ships Ships of the same type and age

traffic Vehicles, such as ships, traveling along a route

training exercise A task carried out to practice and improve skills

unsolved When there is no answer to a problem or puzzle

waterspout A funnel-shaped whirling column of air and water

yacht A light sailing boat used for racing or pleasure trips

Index

Further Reading

• Donkin, Andrew. *Bermuda Triangle*, DK Eyewitness Readers: Level 3.
DK Publishing, 2000.

• Oxlade, Chris. *Mystery of the Bermuda Triangle*, "Can Science Solve?"
series. Heinemann Library, 2007.

• Rudolph, Aaron L. *The Bermuda Triangle*, "The Unexplained" series.
Edge Books, 2004.

• Wallace, Holly. *The Mystery of Atlantis*, "Can Science Solve?" series.
Heinemann Library, 2006.

Printed in the U.S.A.